Silver Link Silk Editions

SLP

The Tramways of Glasgow – 1956

First published in Great Britain in 2025
by Silver Link Books
an imprint of Mortons Books Ltd
Media Centre
Morton Way
Horncastle LN9 6JR
www.mortonsbooks.co.uk

Copyright © Silver Link Books 2025

All rights reserved. No part of this publication may be reproduced or transmitted in any form or by any means, electronic or mechanical including photocopying, recording, or any information storage retrieval system without prior permission in writing from the publisher.

ISBN 978 1 85794 581 2

The right of Henry Conn to be identified as the author of this work has been asserted in accordance with the Copyright, Designs and Patents Act 1988.

Front cover: At Paisley Cross is Coronation 1283 new in 1940; in the background is the two tower Paisley Town Hall, designed by W H Lynn of Belfast, work started in 1879 and the official opening was on 30 January 1882. The statue is of George Aitken Clark, a thread manufacturer in Paisley, who donated £60,000 to build the town hall. *David Clarke*

Back cover: At five past five on 6 July David is at the Cross Stobs terminus of the service 14 to the university. This is round dash Standard 928, new in 1900. *David Clarke*

ACKNOWLEDGMENTS

This is the fourth book in a series that features the wonderful views of David and John Clarke taken in the year 1956. I have, in a number of previous books, featured a large number from David's collection, not so many from John's. I most sincerely thank David and John for access to their rare and wonderful collection of negatives and slides. Note that all the views, never before published, are in chronological order.

Silver Link Silk Editions

SLP

THE TRAMWAYS OF GLASGOW – 1956

Henry Conn

INTRODUCTION

By the mid-1920s the Glasgow tram system was carrying the population of Glasgow quickly and cheaply over track kept in first class condition. It was possible to travel over 20 miles from Airdrie to Elderslie or nearly 23 miles from Milngavie to Renfrew Ferry and at that time the fleet strength was over 1,000 trams, most of which were of a 'Standard' design that had been progressively modernised over the years.

The early Thirties witnessed the closure of a tram route in Paisley. This was of little significance then, but it was the beginning of the end of trams in Glasgow. It should be noted, however, in the middle Thirties new sections of track were opened to Milngavie, west of Anniesland Cross and near to the exhibition site at Bellahouston.

The same period saw the continuation and final completion of the modernisation of the Standard cars. By 1937, however, the youngest of these cars was 13 years old and many had seen service for 40 years.

In 1937 the first of 150 new streamline trams began to enter service. Called 'Exhibition Cars' to begin with, they soon became known as 'Coronation Cars'. They were comfortable, fast, built with heating and forced ventilation, loudspeakers and leather upholstery. The lack of opening windows caused problems in very hot weather as the forced ventilation could not cope.

In 1940, experimental cars 1001 to 1004 were built by GCT at the Coplawhill Tramcar Works, and they were slightly larger than the Standards and 3ft shorter than the Coronations. The Coronations cost £3,354 each in 1938 and the average cost of the experimental cars was £700 less. No. 1001 was built in October 1939, No. 1002 in Nov, and Nos. 1003/4 in January 1940. Their seating was 24/38 (1001) and 24/36 (1002-4); all ran on EMB or Maley & Taunton four-wheel trucks. There was a separate driver cab, leather upholstered seats in both saloons, sliding Pullman passenger doors, and even a step light. One more appeared in 1943 but mounted on a Brush 21E truck. With the closure of Paisley services in May 1957 they moved to Govan Depot where they worked the shipyard rush hour services for just a year before moving to Newlands Depot. They were not used operationally while there and returned to Govan when Newlands closed. In February 1959 they were sold to Connell's of Coatbridge for scrap.

Another experimental car was built in 1947, 1005, and was originally built as a unidirectional car with front entrance and rear exit with Vambac control equipment. This was later rebuilt to the normal pattern with full controls at both ends; the Vambac equipment was removed.

Between 1948 and 1952 a hundred new trams were delivered, the majority in 1950. Coronation MkII was widely used as their name, and so was Cunarder. The Cunarder was not as popular as the Coronation as the platform step was much higher from the road and very tall people said that the seats were too close together and there was no room for their knees. To begin with they tended to roll; later modifications to the suspension help alleviate this however. The Cunarders were the largest trams ever built in Glasgow but were not as large as the Liverpool trams.

The Liverpool trams, 'Green Goddesses' were purchased for £500 each and entered service between 1953 and 1956. They were not popular, but the purchase price was a fraction of the cost of a new tram; with the end of the trams just a few years away they were considered a good buy although maintaining them caused considerable difficulties.

The views in this book feature all the types of trams mentioned above. Additionally, there were 50 bogie double deck cars, known as Kilmarnock Bogies, dating from the late 1920s, used on routes which lasted to the end, so not featured here as most of the views concentrate on routes closed in 1956 and 1957.

By 1950 around 75% of the cars in the Corporation fleet were over 35 years old and much of the plant and equipment was far from new. There was a profit with the trams in 1954, but during and after the war the tracks drifted into disrepair through lack of labour, materials and with rising costs it was becoming no longer economic to renovate them.

Enjoy the nostalgia...

The Tramways of Glasgow – 1956

The first view taken by John was just after midday on 4 July at Airdrie of 1193, a Coronation car, new in 1938, indicating Anderston Cross, via Parkhead as its destination. *John Clarke*

Arriving at Airdrie terminus at 12.10pm is hex dash Standard car 20, on the local Airdrie to Coatbridge service. This usually showed a blank route number indicator, but car 20 appears to be showing quite a bit of 30. *John Clarke*

In Graham Street Airdrie is Coronation car 1147, which was one of the first eight Coronations built by Glasgow Corporation in 1937. All depots received an allocation of the Coronation cars. *John Clarke*

At Airdrie East Station at 12.36pm is Coronation 1153 new in 1938; the station closed on 3 May 1943 but it remained open as a goods depot and the site today is a car park. In the distance is a SMT AEC Regent III. *John Clarke*

The Tramways of Glasgow – 1956

Passing the entrance to Queen Victoria Street in Airdrie at 12.44pm is car 20. The van to the left of this view is a Morris PV van and this was Morris's first forward control van; the older vans can be distinguished from later models by the horizontal split in the driver's side of the windscreen. *David Clarke*

The Tramways of Glasgow – 1956

Coatbridge Depot had a capacity for 21 cars and closed when the trams to Airdrie ceased on 3 November 1956. On the last day of operation car 1251 operated the last passenger tram into Airdrie from Glasgow and was prepared to operate the last tram in Airdrie and Coatbridge. 1251 left at 1.02am and ran to Baillieston, arriving at 1.32am, where it reversed and returned to the Coatbridge depot for the last time. After this date route 15 was cut back to Baillieston. *John Clarke*

The Tramways of Glasgow – 1956

On Main Street east of Dunbeth Road is Coronation 1172 new in 1938. Note the Milanda bakery van; Milanda Bakery, Victoria Bread and Biscuit Works in Wesleyan Street, Glasgow was, by 1974, operated as Milanda bakery. It closed shortly after and was quickly demolished; the site has since been redeveloped for housing. *John Clarke*

In Main Street Coatbridge at its junction with Jackson Street at 1.17pm is car 20; Littlewoods' pools success inspired many others, including Manchester department store owner Vernon Sangster, who comes up with a rival football pool. He partnered with George Randall Kennerley, a Wirral-based businessman, to create Vernons' Pools in Liverpool. *David Clarke*

Passing under Coatbridge Central railway bridge at 1.32pm is Coronation 1183 new in 1938. A busy road scene but very few pedestrians. In the opposite direction is BB59, (FFS 180), an Alexander bodied AEC Regent III new in March 1948 and sold in May 1968. Ahead of BB59 is Baxter's Bus Service 7, (CWY 217), an all Leyland TS8 new to Todmorden Corporation in 1938 and acquired by Baxter's in 1951 and purchased by a showman in 1959. *John Clarke*

West of the Coatbridge Central railway bridge at 1.40pm is Coronation 1180 with another Coronation, 1233, in the background; both were new in 1938. The Coatbridge railway bridges were built in 1898 by the Caledonian Railway Company and Brandon Bridge Company. *John Clarke*

Heading east in Bank Street, Coatbridge, at 1.44pm towards Airdrie is Coronation 1251 new in 1939; during the war many of the Coronations had their seating altered to increase standing room, but all were changed back to the normal seating arrangement in 1947. There seems to be a sizeable queue awaiting the next car heading west. *John Clarke*

At West End Park in Coatbridge heading away from the camera into the city is Coronation car 1184 new in 1938; the Albion lorry belongs to Hugh Harper of Armadale. *John Clarke*

Looking west along the reserved track at 2.14pm in the afternoon heading for Airdrie is Coronation car 1145, another of the first eight built by Glasgow Corporation in 1937. *John Clarke*

At 2.18pm Coronation car 1180, new in 1938, is near the beginning of the reserved track. The roadside reserved track between Baillieston and Langloan was built in 1923. *David Clarke*

The Tramways of Glasgow – 1956

Another view of Coronation car 1180, on the reserved track at 2.18pm looking east. *John Clarke*

Looking west on the reserved track on route 15 is the rear of 1180, seen approaching in the previous view. The SMT bus in the background is J59 (CSF 260), an all Leyland TD5 which was new in April 1939 and which was renumbered HH59 in October 1956. It was sold in December 1957. *John Clarke*

The Tramways of Glasgow – 1956

In Bargeddie, heading for Airdrie, just after crossing the B757 road is Coronation car 1153 new in 1938. *John Clarke*

At Bargeddie Post Office at 2.37pm in the afternoon is Coronation car 1163, new in 1938. Just visible in the background is an SMT AEC Regal. *John Clarke*

The Tramways of Glasgow – 1956

It is now 4.26pm in the afternoon of 4 July and this is hex dash Standard 74 at Hyndland Station; Glasgow did not have automatic bow collector reversers so the conductor had to lean out and pull the rope that is just visible in the top window and over the route number blind. *John Clarke*

At the junction of Hyndland Road and Great Western Road at 4.40pm working service 5 is Coronation car 1168, new in 1938. *David Clarke*

The Tramways of Glasgow – 1956

Near Queensborough Gardens at 4.53pm is round dash Standard car 360, which was originally constructed in 1904; a wonderful view of Glasgow tenements and the gable ends of these were a favourite place for advertisements, although the gable end in this view is strangely devoid of advertisements. *John Clarke*

At the junction of Clarence Drive with Hyndland Road working service 24 at 5pm in the early evening are Coronations 1146, new in 1937, and 1215, which was new the following year. *John Clarke*

On Hyndland Road at its junction with North Gardner Street at 5.03pm is round dash Standard 400. The Standard trams had undergone rebuilds and annual overhauls to keep them going; 400 in 1956 was 52 years in service. *John Clarke*

Five minutes later, at Highburgh Road at its junction with Dowanhill Street working a 24 is Coronation 1241 new in 1939. The worst feature of the Coronations was the absence of opening windows and the reliance on fans for ventilation which led, on warm days, to both saloons becoming very hot.
John Clarke

The last featured view taken on 4 July at 5.11pm is at Highburgh Road between the junctions of Dowanhill Street and Beaumont Gate. Working a 24 is round dash Standard 602 which was originally constructed in 1901. The Glasgow Corporation bus is B55 (FYS 272), a Roberts bodied Albion CX37S new in March 1950 and sold after only 11 years' service in March 1961. *John Clarke*

At Bridge Street at 11.30am on 5 July, working a 5, is 445, a round dash Standard car originally constructed in 1902. In comparison, working an 8, is 88, a hex dash Standard car new in the early 1920s. There are rear views of a Hillman Minx and a Morris Minor and on the right of the view a later manufactured Morris PV. *John Clarke*

Meanwhile David is at Langside depot and entering at 11.41am is round dash Standard car 617. When Langside depot closed a couple of months later service 12 was wholly operated by Govan depot and the portion of service 5 operated by Langside was transferred to Newlands depot. *David Clarke*

Just after midday this is Coronation car 1241, new in 1939, showing the scissors crossover at Battlefield Road near Langside depot. Cars on service 5 turn right into Holmlea Road. The van to the right of the view I think is a 1940s Commer Van. *David Clarke*

It is 12.13pm and John is at Arden boundary and working route 14 is car 665, a hex dash Standard car new in 1923. On 29 September the service to Cross Stobs was withdrawn and all the cars from the university terminated at Arden. Note the British Road Services articulated lorry behind which is a Bedford O type. *John Clarke*

Passing the works of Lawrence Scott Electro Motors Limited on the reserved track at Arden at 12.17pm is 1396, one of six built in 1954 with a Coronation style body on ex Liverpool trucks. *John Clarke*

On Queens Drive at 1.08pm David has taken this view of round dash Standard car 779 which was new in 1900; 779 is now in Glasgow's Riverside Museum and has been rebuilt and preserved in the red route livery, representing the trams that could be found working around 1910. *David Clarke*

Working service 5 at the junction of Victoria Road and Allison Street at 1.29pm is Coronation car 1223, new in 1938. Note the Morris Minor and Morris Minor Traveller on the other side of the road. *David Clarke*

John is now in Barrhead at 1.35pm and working a 14 is 1256, a 1939 Coronation; the lorry is a 1950 Glasgow-registered Atkinson belonging to McCallum & Munro Potato Merchants; note that only two ropes near the rear hold this load onto the lorry. *John Clarke*

A divergence, on Main Street Barrhead at 2.10pm at its junction with Bank Street heading for Neilston, providing a contrast to the trams, this is MD491 (BCS 341), a Newton Mearns allocated all Leyland PD1 new in 1947. *John Clarke*

This is Coronation car 1217, new in 1938, at the junction of Eglinton Street and Devon Street at 2.12pm. The parked car to the right of 1217 is an Austin A30; the Austin A35 would replace the very successful A30 in 1956. *David Clarke*

Also in Main Street Barrhead, 20 minutes after the Western SMT Leyland PD1, working service 14, is round dash Standard 839, which was originally constructed in 1900. *John Clarke*

A minute later this is the last featured view of John's on 5 July. Cunarder 1306, new in 1949, is passing a 1930s Albion lorry owned by McDonald and first registered in Sunderland; the two-letter code ran out in the early 1930s and the three serial letters were introduced in 1932 as necessary. *John Clarke*

The Tramways of Glasgow – 1956

In Jamaica Street at 3.10pm David has taken this view of No. 39, a sand wagon on a Brill truck which conveyed dry sand to the depots. *David Clarke*

At Millerston terminus at 3.43pm is Cunarder 1359, new in 1950; looks like the weather is a bit dreich with the young lad getting his raincoat put on.
David Clarke

The last featured view of David's on 5 July is this of Cunarder 1376, new in 1951, on Cumbernauld Road at Hogganfield Loch at 4pm. *David Clarke*

David's first view on 6 July is at 10.20am is of two unidentified cars at the junction of Jamaica Street and Argyle Street. *David Clarke*

An hour and ten minutes later and David is at the junction of Duke Street and Belgrove Street taking this view of Cunarder car 1374 new in 1951. Also in view are a Bedford O type lorry, a Central SMT Leyland and yet another Morris PV van. *David Clarke*

The first feature view of John's taken on 6 July is inside Elderslie Depot at 11.42am. This is round dash Standard 290, probably withdrawn and being used for spares. Elderslie was the main depot of the former Paisley system and had a relatively small capacity of 47 trams and closed on 11 May 1957. *John Clarke*

About to pass under the railway bridge at Elderslie at 11.51am this is 1266, a 1939 Coronation car; the view is almost smothered in advertising including two adverts for polo mints and fruit polos. *John Clarke*

At just after midday David is taking this view at Bridgeton Cross of Cunarder car 1387, new in 1951, coming out of James Street. *David Clarke*

A minute later David captures Cunarder car 1356, new in 1950, at Bridgeton Cross, turning from London Road into Main Street. The van in view is an Austin LD which was introduced from December 1954 and produced at Adderley Park in Birmingham. *David Clarke*

In James Street at 12.05pm is Cunarder car 1340 new in 1950. The car facing the camera is a Vauxhall and the lorry just behind is an Austin Loadstar which were produced between 1949 and 1956. *David Clarke*

Paisley, Wellmeadow Street with the clock tower in the background showing 12.20pm this is Cunarder 1367, new in 1950; the lorry in the distance is an elderly Albion. *John Clarke*

At the junction of Ballater Street and Commercial Road at 12.20pm is Cunarder car 1360 new in 1950. The car behind 1360 is, I think, a very new Ford Consul Mark II which cost £781 when new in 1956. *David Clarke*

At Paisley Cross at 12.29pm is hex dash Standard 225; note the Burton's shop to the left in the High Street, with Art Deco buildings designed mostly by Henry Wilson. These were often built to incorporate dance halls or billiard halls on the upper floor, as a way of attracting customers. *John Clarke*

At 12.39pm working a 28 to Sandyford this is hex dash Standard car 103. Unveiled in 1924 the World War 1 Monument at Paisley Cross is topped by a bronze statue named 'The Spirit of the Crusaders' which portrays soldiers from the Western Front accompanied by a medieval knight on horseback. Its inscription reads "To the glorious memory of the 1,953 men of Paisley who gave their lives in the Great War." *John Clarke*

At Glenfield at 12.53pm is Coronation car 1272 new in 1939. Behind 1272 is Western SMT 484 (BCS 334), an all Leyland PD1 new in 1947. *John Clarke*

At one minute past one, hex dash Standard car 182 is on Caplethill Road at Glenburn Road. The chimney in the background is at the factory which was called Glenfield Scouring Works and was founded in the 1820s as a bleachworks, and largely rebuilt in 1879. It was latterly owned by William Fulton & Sons Ltd, scourers, dyers and finishers, who used soft water from the Gleniffer Braes in their processing; the factory closed in March 1966. *John Clarke*

Looking north on Caplethill Road, with Southfield Avenue to the left, is a rear view of 182. *John Clarke*

On Neilston Road at its junction with Thornly Park Avenue at 1.08pm is hex dash Standard car 146; 146 was fitted with a Fischer bow collector for tests on the Mount Florida to Paisley Road Toll experimental section in 1927. *John Clarke*

The Tramways of Glasgow – 1956

At 1.22pm on Neilston Road with Mary Street to the right, is hex dash Standard car 184. I really like this view, considering how devoid it is of traffic there is plenty going on; the council road cleaner is doing a grand job. *John Clarke*

Fifteen minutes after the last view and car 184 has been to Glenfield and back on route 28. We are still on Neilston Road, but now at its junction with Orr Street. Just ahead is McGill's (CHS 355), a Guy Arab new in 1945 and rebodied by Massey in 1955. *John Clarke*

At 1.45pm car 1277, another of the 1940 Coronations, is on Neilston Street with Espedair Street to the right of the view. The Western SMT bus is Newton Mearns allocated MD351, (BCS 312), an all Leyland PD1 new in 1947. *John Clarke*

South of Paisley Cross on Causeyside Street is Coronation 1279, new in 1940; Benzie's is in view with further along McArthur tailors, and there was another Co-op behind 1279 which was clothes and a chemist at different times. The van is a Ford Thames 300E produced between 1954 and 1961. This particular one was first registered in London. *John Clarke*

At 2.05pm at Gilmour Street Station this is Coronation 1270, new in 1939. Note the advertisement on the bridge advertising Jean MacGregor scotch broth, which was produced at the Hillington Industrial Estate. The first and largest industrial estate of its kind in Scotland, Hillington set new standards in the design and provision of industrial and commercial premises. Set up in 1934 by an Act of Parliament, it was designated a 'special area' in response to the depression of the 1930s. Building work started in 1937 and a year later 84 factories had been let. *John Clarke*

On Renfrew Road at 2.17pm at its junction with Niddry Street is hex dash Standard car **184** on a short working heading for the crossover at Lochfield Road. *John Clarke*

This is hex dash Standard 146 at Paisley North, near Glencairn Street, at 2.34pm heading north towards the ferry. When this view was taken, 146 would have been in service for 46 years. *John Clarke*

Ten minutes after the previous view this is hex dash Standard 184 on Paisley Road at its junction with Stewart Avenue. Route 28 was introduced on 15 August 1943 and ran between Renfrew Ferry and Spiersbridge. On 3 April 1949 the route became Renfrew Ferry and Potterhill or Glenfield and the route was abandoned on 11 May 1957. *John Clarke*

At the junction of Paisley Road and Porterfield Road at 3pm, working a service 4, is hex dash Standard 240. On 11 May 1957 the Renfrew and Paisley section of route 4 was abandoned and all cars from Springburn terminated at Hillington Road. *John Clarke*

At the same time as John's view on Paisley Road, Renfrew, David is taking this view of Cunarder 1303, new in 1949, on the reserved track at Arden. The 100 Cunarder trams were a post-war development of the Coronation trams and were amongst the last double-deck trams to be built in the UK, between 1948 and 1952. Though comfortable, they were not regarded as being as reliable or capable as the Coronation trams. *David Clarke*

The Tramways of Glasgow – 1956

On Paisley Road in Renfrew, south of the junction with Glebe Street, at 3.11pm is hex dash Standard 37. The large van is a Bedford A2 and Harvo was a brand of malt loaf made in Birmingham produced until the company went bust in 1973. *John Clarke*

On the High Street in Renfrew at 3.15pm working a 4 is Cunarder 1380, one of 22 Cunarders constructed in 1951; the 1955 Dundee registered van is a Bedford CA. *John Clarke*

At 3.21pm, Coronation 1272, new in 1939, is just south of the terminus at Renfrew Ferry. Looming large in the background is Yoker power station. This was built in 1905 by the British Thomson Houston Co, with equipment supplied by Westinghouse. It was later acquired by the Clyde Valley Electric Power Co, and, in 1955, by the South of Scotland Electricity Board. Output rose from 4000 kilowatts in 1905 to 100,000 kilowatts by 1966, when the coal fired station had eight high-pressure boilers. Today, nothing is visible of Yoker Power Station, which closed in 1976, with its site now occupied by housing. *John Clarke*

Another view of Coronation 1272 with in the background the Orchard vaults and hidden by the tram is the old Regal restaurant, now part of Cottons bar. There is a stone butt from the old railway bridge still standing there today. If you look under the bridge you will see the old prefabs. The bridge once carried the railway which came from Cardonald via Braehead. *John Clarke*

At Renfrew Ferry terminus at 3.26pm in the afternoon are two Coronations with nearest the camera 1266 new in 1939, and behind 1274 new in 1940; it looks to me as if the two young lads have just finished school and have decided to go fishing. *John Clarke*

Fifteen minutes later John is in the High Street at Renfrew, and working a 4 to Springburn is round dash Standard 490 which was originally constructed in 1902. *John Clarke*

Passing an entrance to Braehead power station at 3.55pm is round dash Standard 374, originally constructed in 1904. Braehead was a coalfired power station closed in 1982 with the concrete shell of the building surviving until the 1990s; the site is now part of the Braehead shopping centre. *John Clarke*

On Renfrew Road looking towards Renfrew, with the Town Hall just in view in the distance, is hex dash Standard 19. The car in view is a Vauxhall Velox. In August 1954 a significant facelift was applied to the Velox; the most obvious of the many cosmetic changes was a new front grille and trafficators being replaced by flashing lights. *John Clarke*

The last view taken by John on 6 July to feature in this book is of round dash Standard 358, originally constructed in 1904, at the Shieldhall Spur at 4.35pm. *John Clarke*

The Tramways of Glasgow – 1956

The last featured view taken by David on 6 July and the time can be clearly seen on Paisley Town Hall clock. During 1940 Glasgow Corporation built four experimental trams, 1001 to 1004, and none of them were identical. Number 1003 seen here at Paisley Cross had an EMB truck, GEC motors and MV controllers. None of the four were particularly liked by staff and by 1951 all were at Elderslie depot and were generally used at peak hours only. All were scrapped in 1959. The Western SMT bus behind 1003 is a 1945 Guy Arab with 1954 Northern Counties bodywork. *David Clarke*

The Tramways of Glasgow – 1956

The first view taken on 7 July to feature in this book is at 9.58am with hex dash Standard car 191 at St Georges Road, with Sauchiehall Street at top left. This photo was taken by David from their bed and breakfast accommodation above the shops. *David Clarke*

This is round dash Standard 496, new in 1902, at Holmlea Road at 10.55am. The car in view is a new Glasgow-registered Vauxhall Velox and in the distance is TB1 (FYS 701), a MCCW bodied BUT 9641T new in March 1949 and sold in March 1965. *John Clarke*

Leaving Holmlea Road at the junction of tracks to Langside depot, working a 5A to Kelvinside, is hex dash Standard 1040, new in 1923; the nearest car is a Gloucestershire-registered Austin A50 new in 1955 and behind using semaphore indicators is an Edinburgh-registered Austin A70 Hereford, new in 1953. *John Clarke*

The inside of Langside depot at 11.09am with Tool Van car No.21 in view; No.21 was constructed in 1905 on a Brill 21E truck. The car in front of No.21 is an Edinburgh-registered Morris new in 1952. *John Clarke*

The Tramways of Glasgow – 1956

On the reserved track on Battlefield Road at its junction with Lochleven Road at 11.33am is round dash Standard 297. The Glasgow Corporation bus is D51, (FYS 479), an Alexander-bodied Daimler CVD6 new in March 1951 and sold in September 1965. The car sandwiched between the two is a 1954 Glasgow-registered Vauxhall Velox. *John Clarke*

At the end of the reserved track on Battlefield Road at 11.37am is 1148, a 1937 Coronation car. The lorry delivering fruit and vegetables is a Glasgow-registered Bedford OY which were produced for the army between 1939 and 1953. Also in view are a 1954 Glasgow-registered Standard 10 and a 1954 Ayrshire-registered Bedford CA van. *John Clarke*

Working route 5 at 11.45am on Grange Road is 1939 Coronation 1258 and in the distance is another Coronation 1221, new in 1938. *John Clarke*

At 11.53am on Langside Road, with Queens Park to the right and the old Victoria Infirmary to the left, is hex dash Standard 85; both top deck passenger and driver are taking great interest in the photographer as 85 heads for Anniesland. *John Clarke*

Outside the Langside Road entrance to the old Victoria Infirmary, working a 24, is round dash Standard 296 which was originally constructed in 1908; the car overtaking 24 is a P3 series Rover which were produced between 1948 and 1949. *John Clarke*

Carrying a goodly load of passengers heading for Mount Florida is round dash Standard 986, built in 1900, at the junction of Allison Street and Victoria Road. *John Clarke*

Looking in the opposite direction, approaching the camera working a 12 to Paisley Road Toll, is round dash Standard 780. The prominent car is a 1955 Glasgow-registered Ford Consul which was produced in large numbers between 1951 and 1956. *John Clarke*

At 12.23pm working route 12 to Paisley Road Toll on Cathcart Road with Albert Road and Crosshill Station in the background, is 986. The successful Brill 21E truck was fitted to the first large batch of Standards built from 1899 onwards, of which 986 was one. In spite of a number of experimental motors the 21E truck remained in constant use until 1962 on most of the Standards. *John Clarke*

On Cathcart Road at Queens Drive at 12.29pm is round dash Standard car 727; the car overtaking 727 is a 1955 Glasgow registered Morris Oxford and the car on the right side of the road is a 1954 Glasgow-registered split screen Morris Minor. *John Clarke*

At the same time David is taking this view of hex dash Standard car 176 on Govan Road at Prince's Dock Gate. Prince's Dock was originally known as Cessnock Dock and built 1893-7 for the Clyde Navigation Trust. The formal opening was performed by the Duchess of York on 10 September 1895. Prince's Dock was infilled and landscaped for Glasgow's Garden Festival of 1988. *David Clarke*

At the same location a couple of minutes later is round dash Standard car 631. *David Clarke*

At 12.40pm John is at the Mount Florida terminus of route 12, with round dash Standard 780, originally constructed in 1900. In the background working route 104 is TD19 (FYS 753), a MCCW-bodied Daimler CTM6 new in February 1950 and sold in December 1962. *John Clarke*

Four minutes later and round dash Standard car 780 is now at Prospecthill Road and just appearing in the opposite direction is another hex dash Standard car, 680 which was built in 1924. *John Clarke*

The Tramways of Glasgow – 1956

At 12.50pm on Govan Road, with Prince's Dock to the right of the view, is round dash Standard car 303 followed by similar 300. For most of its life, Prince's dock handled vast quantities of coal for export, but by the 1950s it was mainly used for general cargos. *David Clarke*

This is a fuller view of hex dash Standard 680, at Paisley Road Toll, taken at 1.05pm. In the background is the Imperial cinema and the film showing is the Monster from the Ocean Floor. The Imperial Cinema was opened on 2 January 1921 by Henry Meiklejohn. Although a conversion of some stables, the resultant cinema was so well designed that it was impossible to determine its rather humble origins. Damaged by fire in March 1952, it was rebuilt, but closed in 1959. It was converted into the Grand Ole Opry Social Club, a unique venue for the city's many country and western fans. *John Clarke*

The Tramways of Glasgow – 1956

Meanwhile David is taking this view of Cunarder car 1386, new in 1951, at 1.09pm at Govan Cross. The tracks in the left foreground were used by the Fairfield Shipyard to access the railway at Govan Goods Yard. *David Clarke*

In Paisley Road at Paisley Road Toll at 1.14pm, nearest the camera working a 7 is hex dash Standard 132, new in 1915, and working a 4 is another hex dash car 1051, new in 1923. Note the third tram track leading to Admiral Street. The bus is A236 (FYS 419), a Weymann-bodied AEC Regent III new in November 1951 remaining in the Corporation fleet until June 1965. *John Clarke*

The Tramways of Glasgow – 1956

This is Cunarder car 1364, new in 1950, in Langlands Road at 1.21pm, about to turn into Golspie Street. *David Clarke*

Exiting Seaward Street into Scotland Street at 1.33pm is round dash Standard car 727 new in 1900; prominent on the billboard are Rowntree's Sunripe Jelly, 'tastes like the fruit itself' and Stergene, which was first introduced in 1948 by the makers of Domestos. Sold initially in brown glass bottles, it was specially designed for washing woollens. *John Clarke*

A number of passengers have alighted from round dash Standard 780 in Shields Road at 1.35pm; behind is one of the 1950s billboard adverts for MacDonalds Munchmallow, made at Hillington in Glasgow. *John Clarke*

At 1.38pm, passing Shields Road station, which was opened in 1870 and closed in 1966, is hex dash Standard car 680 which was new in 1924. In the opposite direction is DS25 (FYS 330), a Glasgow Corporation bodied Daimler CVD6 new in February 1951 and sold in December 1964. Between 1948 and 1952 a total of 43 Daimler chassis were bodied at Larkfield and one of the primary duties of this batch was to serve Hillington Industrial Estate because of a restrictive low bridge under the main railway to Paisley. *John Clarke*

Looking north on Shields Road at its junction with Bruce Road at 1.45pm is round dash Standard 986; the car is a 1954 Renfrewshire-registered Ford Anglia 100E. The noticeable differences between a 1950s Ford Anglia and Ford Prefect is that the Prefect had vertical radiator bars and four doors. *John Clarke*

At 2.21pm, 986 is in Nithsdale Road at its junction with Darnley Street to the right. The car is a 1955 Glasgow-registered Austin A50. *John Clarke*

The Tramways of Glasgow – 1956

At 4.01pm John is taking this view of round dash Standard 555 turning from Langlands Road into Golspie Street. Route 7, was replaced by trolleybus service 106, on 14 June 1958. To the left of the tram, visible are the cranes of the Fairfield shipyard. The car to the left of this view is a Birmingham-registered Rover 10 new in 1936. *John Clarke*

A hex dash Standard 668, which was one of a batch of 21 built new between 1923 and 1924, in Elder Street at its junction with Crossloan Road shortly after the previous view. Hopefully the young lad will catch the tram. *John Clarke*

At 4.10pm this is Cunarder car **1368**, one of 53 Cunarders built in **1950**, in Craigton Road. Looking very smart, I think, and ready to hit the town is the lady on the right of this view. Also noteworthy, the motorbike and sidecar combination driver has no helmet. *John Clarke*

Meanwhile, David is in Paisley North at 4.27pm and working route 28 on 7 July is Coronation 1282 new in 1940; all operations of routes in Paisley and Renfrew came to an end on the night of 11 May 1957 and the services were replaced the next day by buses of the Scottish Bus group. *David Clarke*

The Tramways of Glasgow – 1956

By 5.52pm John has travelled the whole length of route 7 from Bellahouston to Millerston, and then back to Bridgeton Cross. Aided by the traffic policeman, hex dash Standard car 40 is turning into James Street while working a 7 to Bellahouston. *John Clarke*

With the acquisition of the independent systems of Airdrie, Coatbridge and Paisley, the Glasgow tram system had some routes deep into the countryside. One of these was the 28 between Renfrew Ferry and Glenfield; the last featured view taken on 7 July by David was at 5.53pm at Glenfield, of Coronation 1271, new in 1940. *David Clarke*

The crowds are building up in this view of Main Street in Cambuslang; it is the 7 July and the time of the year for the orange parade which will pass by in the next five minutes. Working a 17 at 6.25pm is round dash Standard 329. *John Clarke*

At 7.05pm in the evening this is round dash Standard 488 which has just passed under the railway bridge on Cambuslang Road; 488, new in 1902, was the last traditional four-wheeler to carry ordinary fare-paying passengers on British streets and is in preservation. *John Clarke*

With the Clyde Paper Co Ltd factory on Cambuslang Road as a backdrop this is a view of 677 at 7.09pm. The Clyde Paper Company Ltd at Rutherglen near Glasgow was established in 1856 producing rag-paper and later became a major producer of newsprint for the newspaper industry and coated papers. In 1878 long fibre paper produced using esparto grass and in 1900 the first coated papers were produced using wood-pulp fibres using the Fourdrinier process. In 1939 a new factory was built to produce coated papers and the Mill had around 650 employees at this time; sadly, the mill closed in 1971. *John Clarke*

A full hour and 20 minutes later John has travelled to Milngavie, where taking on passengers to Tollcross is round dash Standard 354, originally constructed in 1904. *John Clarke*

The last featured view taken by John on 7 July is of ex Liverpool 1029 arriving at Milngavie at 8.31pm in the evening; this section of the route between Maryhill and Milngavie would last operate on 3 November. The first batch of 25 Liverpool trams were acquired in 1953 and were fast, smooth riding and comfortable but had limited route availability due to their greater width than Glasgow cars. *John Clarke*

Back in Glasgow on 13 July, turning from Byres Road into Church Street, working route 5 at 12.47pm this is round dash Standard 702. In the background is a Scammell Scarab in which the engine was mounted lower and more centrally than in the Mechanical Horse, making the Scarab much more stable. The railways, for which this style of vehicle was originally designed continued to be a primary customer, although there were many other users, the manoeuvrability proving popular for companies operating in city environments. *John Clarke*

David's first featured view on 13 July at 1.49pm is 1005 in Maryhill Road near the Killermont Golf Club. Car 1005 was built as an experimental single ended tram and its unusual front entrance loading arrangements made 1005 unpopular with the Glasgow public amongst a fleet of more than a thousand orthodox trams. Also it was limited to the few circular routes, so was rebuilt to double ended resembling the Cunarders. *David Clarke*

In Byres Road at 1.52pm, at its junction with Ruthven Street, this is **1938** Coronation car 1221. The gleaming car is a **1955** Glasgow registered Rover 90 which had a 2.6 litre engine with a top speed of 90mph with a fuel consumption of 20.3 miles per gallon. *John Clarke*

Another view of 1005 taken at Maryhill at 2pm by David. In an attempt to make better use of 1005 it entered the workshops during 1955 for a rebuild that dispensed with the single ended arrangement. A driver's cab and full controls were provided in the rear. The work was carried out on a strict budget and, although successful in making 1005 more standardised, it still saw only infrequent use generally appearing only during rush hour period until 1962 when it was finally withdrawn and disposed of for scrap. *David Clarke*

On Byers Road at 2.04pm with the Botanic Gardens in the background this is round dash Standard 702, which was originally constructed in 1899, and unusually had a EMB flexible axle truck. The gardens were originally used for concerts and other events, and in 1891 the gardens were incorporated into the Parks and Gardens of the City of Glasgow. *John Clarke*

Just under an hour later, at 3pm, John is on Maryhill Road just north of Maryhill Park taking this view of ex Liverpool 1014 which had M & T swing link bogies with a 4ft 3in wheelbase. *John Clarke*

On Milngavie Road at 3.10pm working service 29, this is round dash Standard 315. The lorry carrying, by the looks of it, potatoes, is not overtaking the car, as I think the car is rather poorly parked on a bend. *John Clarke*

On Milngavie Road close to its junction with Ferguston Road at 3.15pm this is ex Liverpool 1014. Glasgow purchased a further 22 Liverpool trams in 1954 but even as these arrived troubles began; with their lack of bulkheads in the lower deck the platforms began to droop. *John Clarke*

At 3.18pm David is on Glasgow Road near Renfrew Airport taking this view of 1377, a Cunarder new in 1951. *David Clarke*

Passing Kessington Road on Milngavie Road at 3.26pm is ex Liverpool 1036 which had EMB lightweight bogies with a wheel base of 4ft 6in. Further problems with the Liverpool trams included rainwater getting into the driving position and constant problems with the electric wiring which led to the wiring being totally renewed. *John Clarke*

At Hillfoot station at 3.38pm is hex dash Standard 33; Hillfoot station was opened on 1 May 1900 and is still operational today. Note the billboard for Mackeson; Mackeson's Brewery of Hythe, Kent, first released the beer in 1909 to celebrate the 240th anniversary of brewing in Hythe and by the 1950s Mackeson accounted for half of Whitbread's output. *John Clarke*

Would it not be fantastic if the roads were as quiet as this. On Paisley Road in Renfrew at 3.50pm is Coronation car 1272 new in 1939. *David Clarke*

Fifteen minutes later David is taking this view in Gilmour Street Paisley of 1282, a Coronation new in 1940. *David Clarke*

The Tramways of Glasgow – 1956

At Wellmeadow Street in Paisley at 4.09pm, this is 1004. Although the Coronations were very highly regarded, they were expensive to build and operate and were not suitable for routes with tight curves, so a cheaper alternative was considered. Four experimental four-wheel cars were built in 1939-40, 1001 to 1004, and more would likely have followed had it not been for the Second World War, which prevented large scale fleet renewal. They spent most of their lives working Paisley area local services, but after the closure of the Paisley routes in 1957 they were mainly used on Govan shipyard workers' extras. *David Clarke*

The Tramways of Glasgow – 1956

Passing Keystone Quadrant on Main Street in Milngavie at 4.09pm is ex Liverpool 1034. The Liverpool trams were normally confined to 15 and 29 because of the relatively easy curves of these two routes. The 29 to and from Milngavie and Maryhill to Tollcross and Broomhouse had, however, several sharp curves in the city centre such as Argyle Street/Hope Street, Hope Street/Cowcaddens and Cowcaddens/New City Road, yet the Liverpool cars managed them with little difficulty. *John Clarke*

Standing in Elderslie depot at 4.17pm is round dash Standard car 833, new in 1900. *David Clarke*

The Tramways of Glasgow – 1956

At Milngavie terminus at 4.22pm this is ex Liverpool 1015; unfortunately, none of the Liverpool trams survived until the end of the Glasgow system with the last scrapped at Coplawhill in July 1960. *John Clarke*

Just a few minutes later in Milngavie is 1005, the unidirectional tram with front entrance and rear exit built in 1947, and later rebuilt to double ended. 1005 was Glasgow's most original tram and it first operated on the circular 33. *John Clarke*

David is in Neilston Road, Paisley, at 4.39pm with Coronation car 1280, new in 1940, about to reverse over Lochfield Road crossover. *David Clarke*

Forty minutes after the last view of 1005 at Milngavie, John is in Argyle Street at the 'Hielanman's Umbrella', the Glaswegian nickname for the glass-walled wide railway bridge which carries the platforms of Glasgow Central station across Argyle Street; I think 1005 looks very smart in this view. *John Clarke*

The Tramways of Glasgow – 1956

A rear end view of 1005 passing Arnott Simpson in Argyle Street; the department stores of Arnott & Co and Robert Simpson & Sons were established in the 1850s. In 1936 at a time of difficult trading conditions in the economic depression of the 1930s, both firms were acquired by the House of Fraser and combined, trading as Arnott Simpson from 1938. Arnott Simpson's was completely rebuilt in the early 1960s, reopening in April 1963. The new building was double the size of the old and became one of Glasgow's leading department stores with a new food hall and departments spread over six floors. *John Clarke*

It is 5.55pm and John is taking this view of Cunarder 1358, new in 1950, followed by Coronation 1281, new in 1940, at Ralston on Glasgow Road, looking towards Paisley. *John Clarke*

In Glasgow Road, Paisley, at 6.04pm, looking towards Glasgow at the entrance to Barshaw Park, is round dash Standard 697; behind 697 is a Ford Zephyr passing an Austin Devon A40, and a Western SMT Guy Arab bus. *John Clarke*

The Tramways of Glasgow – 1956

At Hawkhead Road is **1340**, a 1950 Cunarder; passing **1340** is a locally-registered Austin A40 Somerset. *John Clarke*

Waiting at the crossover east of Hawkhead Road is 1003 one of the experimental streamlined 'Lightweight' cars built by GCT at the Coplawhill Tramcar Works. *John Clarke*

Approaching Paisley Town Hall from the east at 6.28pm is 1361, a 1950 Cunarder; note the Galbraith's Stores in the background. Galbraith's Stores' first shop was established at the corner of Bridge Street and Napier Street in Linwood Village, Paisley in 1894. Within six years the company had 12 stores and had expanded to over 59 shops by 1919. The store network grew rapidly and by 1939 the company had over 159 grocery branches and 12 butcher's shops. Along with a 'provisions' window, staple items such as tea, sugar and bakery goods were advertised with the emphasis on price. The stores were originally served by a single warehouse, in Paisley. As the store network grew a second warehouse was added in Glasgow closely followed by a third warehouse in Govan, Glasgow. Manufacturing was a key success to their growth. By owning their manufacturing, the company increased profitability and secured supplies to its stores. The company established a bakery in 1895 at George Street, Paisley to supply its own stores. By 1911 a second bakery was added in Govan to supply the Glasgow branches. The company was acquired in 1954 by Home and Colonial Stores for £2,340,000. By this time the store network had expanded to over 220 stores and was regarded as the leading independent grocery business in the west of Scotland. *John Clarke*

The last view in this book at Paisley Town Hall was taken by John on 13 July at 6.29pm; nearest the camera is 1370, a 1951 Cunarder with 1361, new in 1950, (seen in the previous view), heading in the opposite direction. *John Clarke*

INDEX

Tram cars					Places	
19	72	617	31	1215	26	1396	34
20	6, 9, 12	631	86	1217	36		
33	119	665	33	1221	81, 112	**Places**	
37	65	668	100	1223	34	Admiral Street	92
39	39	677	107	1233	14	Airdrie	4-7, 9, 10, 15, 17, 21, 104
40	103	680	88, 90, 96	1241	28, 32	Airdrie East Station	8
74	23	697	130	1251	10, 15	Albert Road	83
85	82	702	110, 114	1256	34	Allison Street	34, 82
88	30	727	84, 94	1258	81	Anderston Cross	5
103	50	779	34	1266	44, 69	Anniesland	82
132	92	780	82, 87, 88, 95	1270	59	Anniesland Cross	4
146	54, 61	833	124	1271	104	Arden	33, 34, 64
176	85	839	37	1272	51, 67, 68, 120	Argyle Street	42, 123, 128, 129
182	52, 53	986	82, 83, 97, 98	1274	69	Baillieston	10, 18
184	55, 56, 60, 62	1001	4, 74, 122	1277	57	Ballater Street	48
191	75	1002	4, 74, 122	1279	58	Bank Street	15, 35
225	49	1003	4, 74, 122, 132	1280	127	Bargeddie	21, 22
240	63	1004	4, 74, 122	1281	130	Barrhead	34, 35, 37
290	44	1005	4, 111, 113, 126, 128, 129	1282	102, 121	Barshaw Park	130
296	82	1014	115, 116	1303	64	Battlefield Road	32, 79, 80
297	79	1015	125	1306	38	Beaumont Gate	29
300	89	1029	109	1340	46, 131	Belgrove Street	43
303	89	1034	123	1356	45	Bellahouston	4, 103
315	116	1036	118	1358	130	Birmingham	45, 65
329	105	1040	77	1359	40	Botanic Gardens	114
354	108	1051	92	1360	48	Braehead	68, 71
358	73	1146	26	1361	133, 134	Bridge Street	30, 133
360	25	1147	7	1364	93	Bridgeton Cross	44, 45, 103
374	71	1148	80	1367	47	Broomhouse	123
400	27	1153	8, 21	1368	101	Byres Road	110, 112
445	30	1163	22	1370	134	Cambuslang Road	106, 107
488	106	1168	24	1374	43	Capelhill Road	52, 53
490	70	1172	11	1376	41	Cardonald	68
496	76	1180	14, 18-20	1377	117	Cathcart Road	83, 84
555	99	1183	13	1380	66	Causeyside Street	58
602	29	1184	16	1386	91	Cessnock Dock	85
		1193	5	1387	44	Church Street	110

Clarence Drive	26	Govan depot	4, 31	London Road	45	Potterhill	62
Coatbridge	4, 6, 10, 12, 15, 16, 104	Govan Goods Yard	91	Main Street Barrhead	35, 37	Prince's Dock Gate	85
Coatbridge Central	13, 14	Govan Road	85, 89	Main Street Bridgeton	45	Prospecthill Road	88
Coatbridge depot	10	Graham Street	7	Main Street Cambuslang	105	Queensborough Gardens	25
Commercial Road	48	Grange Road	81	Main Street Coatbridge	11, 12	Queens Drive	34, 84
Coplawhill Tramcar Works	4, 125, 132	Great Western Road	24	Main Street Milngavie	123	Queens Park	82
Cowcaddens	123	Hawkhead Road	131, 132	Manchester	12	Queen Victoria Street	9
Craigton Road	101	Highburgh Road	28, 29	Maryhill	109, 113, 123	Renfrew	63-65, 70, 72, 102, 120
Crosshill Station	83	Hillfoot station	119	Maryhill Park	115	Renfrew Airport	117
Crossloan Road	100	Hillington	95	Maryhill Road	111, 115	Renfrew Ferry	4, 62, 67, 69, 104
Cross Stobs	2, 33	Hillington Industrial Estate	59, 96	Mary Street	55	Renfrew High Street	66
Cumbernauld Road	41	Hillington Road	63	Milanda Bakery	11	Renfrew Road	60, 72
Darnley Street	98	Hogganfield Loch	41	Millerston terminus	40, 103	Riverside Museum	34
Devon Street	36	Holmlea Road	32, 76, 77	Milngavie	4, 108, 109, 123, 125, 126, 128	Rutherglen	107
Dowanhill Street	28, 29	Hope Street	123	Milngavie Road	116, 118	Ruthven Street	112
Duke Street	43	Hyndland Road	24, 26, 27	Mount Florida	54, 82, 87	Sandyford	50
Dunbeth Road	11	Hyndland Station	23	Napier Street	133	Sauchiehall Street	75
Edinburgh	77, 78	Hythe, Kent	119	Neilston	35	Scotland Street	94
Eglinton Street	36	Imperial cinema	90	Neilston Road	54-56, 127	Seaward Street	94
Elderslie	4, 44	Jackson Street	12	Neilston Street	57	Shieldhall Spur	73
Elderslie depot	44, 74, 124	Jamaica Street	39, 42	New City Road	123	Shields Road	95, 97
Elder Street	100	James Street	44, 46, 103	Newlands depot	4, 31	Shields Road Station	96
Espedair Street	57	Kelvinside	77	Newton Mearns	35, 57	Southfield Avenue	53
Fairfield Shipyard	91, 99	Kessington Road	118	Niddry Street	60	Spiersbridge	62
Ferguston Road	116	Keystone Quadrant	123	Nithsdale Road	98	Springburn	63, 70
George Street	133	Killermont Golf Club	111	North Gardner Street	27	Stewart Avenue	62
Gilmour Street	121	Langlands Road	93, 99	Orchard vaults	68	St Georges Road	75
Gilmour Street station	59	Langloan	18	Orr Street	56	Thornly Park Avenue	54
Glasgow Road	117, 130	Langside depot	31, 32, 77, 78	Paisley	2, 4, 44, 47, 50, 63, 96, 102, 104, 121, 122, 127, 130, 133	Tollcross	108, 123
Glebe Street	65	Langside Road	82			Victoria Infirmary	82
Glenburn Road	52	Larkfield	96	Paisley Cross	2, 49, 50, 58, 74	Victoria Road	34
Glencairn Street	61	Linwood Village	133	Paisley North	61, 102	Wellmeadow Street	47, 122
Glenfield	51, 56, 62, 104	Liverpool	4, 12, 34, 109, 115, 116, 118, 123, 125	Paisley Road	62-65, 92, 120	Wesleyan Street	11
Glenfield Scouring Works	52			Paisley Road Toll	54, 82, 83, 90, 92	West End Park	16
Golspie Street	93, 99	Lochfield Road	60, 127	Paisley Town Hall	2, 74, 133, 134	Wirral	12
Govan	4, 122, 133	Lochleven Road	79	Parkhead	5	Yoker power station	67
Govan Cross	91	London	58	Porterfield Road	63